New Caribbean Junior Reader

Revised Edition

Diane Browne   Peggy Campbell

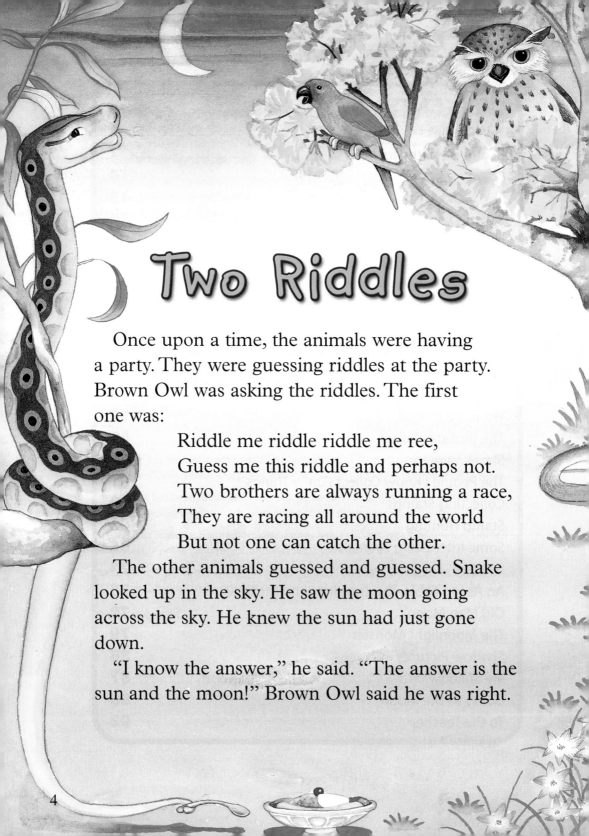

Two Riddles

Once upon a time, the animals were having a party. They were guessing riddles at the party. Brown Owl was asking the riddles. The first one was:

> Riddle me riddle riddle me ree,
> Guess me this riddle and perhaps not.
> Two brothers are always running a race,
> They are racing all around the world
> But not one can catch the other.

The other animals guessed and guessed. Snake looked up in the sky. He saw the moon going across the sky. He knew the sun had just gone down.

"I know the answer," he said. "The answer is the sun and the moon!" Brown Owl said he was right.

The second riddle was:

> Riddle me this and riddle me that,
> Guess me this riddle and perhaps not.
> Rain is coming.
> There are two empty rooms,
> But you cannot go in them.

The animals looked at one another.
Monkey looked at his friend, Tiger. He looked at his nose. Then he smiled and said, "I know the answer. It is a nose!" Brown Owl said he was right.

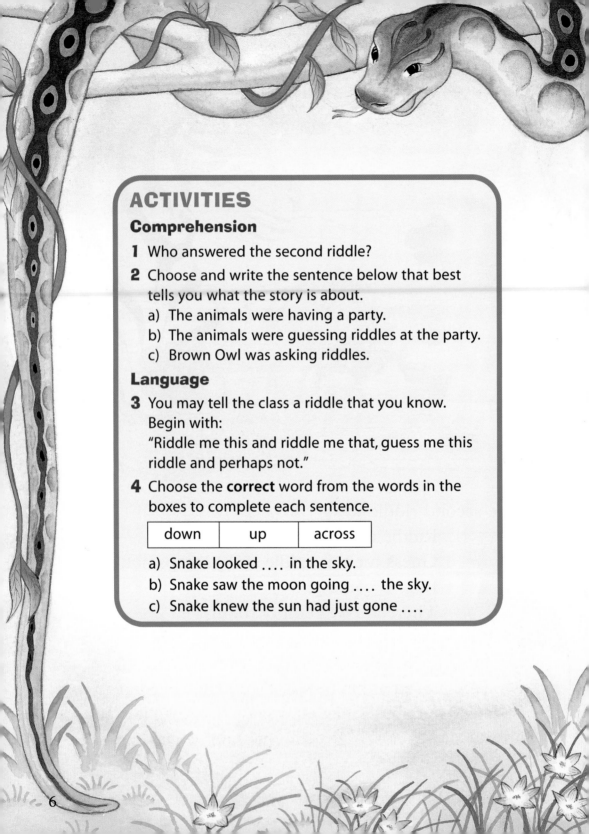

ACTIVITIES

Comprehension

1 Who answered the second riddle?

2 Choose and write the sentence below that best tells you what the story is about.
  a) The animals were having a party.
  b) The animals were guessing riddles at the party.
  c) Brown Owl was asking riddles.

Language

3 You may tell the class a riddle that you know. Begin with:
  "Riddle me this and riddle me that, guess me this riddle and perhaps not."

4 Choose the **correct** word from the words in the boxes to complete each sentence.

down	up	across

  a) Snake looked .... in the sky.
  b) Snake saw the moon going .... the sky.
  c) Snake knew the sun had just gone ....

Big for Me, Little for You

At the party, the animals were telling crick-crack stories. Snake told the first story because he had guessed the first riddle.

He started the story in the way that all crick-crack stories start. He said,

"Crick-crack."

All the animals shouted,

"Break my back."

Then Snake told his story.

Once upon a time, Tiger and Rabbit were friends. One day Rabbit asked Tiger to go with him to catch fish. He told her they would have a good time and catch a lot of big fish to eat. Tiger thought this would be good fun. So the two friends went down to the beach and let down their fishing lines.

As they were fishing Tiger said, "Big for me, little for you."

"What did you say, Tiger?" asked Rabbit in surprise.

"Big for me, little for you," Tiger said again.

"But that is not fair," said Rabbit. "You must be fair. Each of us should get a fair share of what we catch."

Tiger opened her mouth so that Rabbit could see her sharp teeth. Then she showed her sharp claws. She looked fierce and dangerous. Then she said again, "Big for me, little for you."

"Of course, of course, Tiger!" Rabbit said. But he was very angry.

Soon the fish started to bite. They caught
plenty of big fish and plenty of little fish.

When it was time to share the fish, Tiger
showed her sharp teeth and claws and looked fierce
and dangerous.

"Big for me, little for you," she said. She put all
the big fish in her basket and all the little ones in
Rabbit's basket.

Rabbit knew this was not fair. He knew he must
work out a way to trick Tiger. So he asked Tiger to
come again the next day. Tiger was very happy.

By the time Rabbit got home he had his trick all worked out. He called his children and told them. Then he painted each one a different colour. He painted them red, blue, green and all different colours.

The next day Tiger and Rabbit went to the beach again. Each time Rabbit caught a big fish, Tiger said with a fierce and dangerous look, "Big for me, little for you." And each time Rabbit caught a little fish Tiger showed her sharp teeth and claws and said, "Little for you, big for me."

Rabbit only said, "Of course, of course, Tiger."

After Tiger shared out the fish, Rabbit said, "I do not feel so well, Tiger. You go on home. I will soon come." So Tiger took up her basket with plenty of big fish and left Rabbit with his basket with plenty of little fish. As Tiger came to the first corner, she saw a little red rabbit in the way. It was on its back with its feet in the air.

"A dead red rabbit," said Tiger, and went on her way.

At the next corner she saw a dead blue rabbit. At the next corner she saw a dead green rabbit. At each corner there was a dead rabbit of a different colour.

At last Tiger stopped and said, "I must be mad. How can I leave all these rabbits? They are not Rabbit's children because they are all different colours. So it can't be a trick. Let me go back for them."

So Tiger put down her basket and ran back for the rabbits. But Rabbit and his children came up quietly and hid in the bushes. And as soon as Tiger put down the basket and left, they grabbed it up and away they went.

As they ran Rabbit said, "All for me, none for you. People must learn to be fair."

And that was the end of Snake's crick-crack story, so to end it he said, "Wire bend."

And all the other animals shouted, "Story end."

ACTIVITIES

Literature

1

| clever | selfish | friendly | greedy |

   a) Which word or words describe Tiger?
   b) Which word or words describe Rabbit?

Language

2 In the story what is meant by:
   a) *looked fierce and dangerous* on page 8, line 11?
   b) *started to bite* on page 9, line 1?

3 brown   low   grow   glow   snow
   flow   town   brow   blow   cow
   tow   down   know   slow   crowd
   a) List the words that have the same '**ow**' sound as in
      'sh**ow**', e.g. fl**ow**.
   b) List the words that have the same '**ow**' sound as in
      'n**ow**' e.g. br**ow**n.

4 Choose the correct word that completes each sentence.
   Write the sentence.
   a) Rabbit can run fast, but Tiger can run . . . .
                                    fast   faster
   b) Sarah dug a deep hole. It was . . . .
                           deep   deeper
      than Debbie's.
   c) Tiger caught some big fish, but Rabbit caught
      . . . . ones.
      big   bigger

POEMS

Poems are the nicest things to read. Poems sound best when you read them aloud. This is because they have a special rhythm. Sometimes you can beat out the rhythm just as if you are playing drums in music.

Poems often have words that are repeated just like the words in a song. Poems often have words that rhyme or words starting with the same letter or the same sound. Words that rhyme and words with the same sounds help us to hear the rhythm.

Poems have words that help you imagine a picture just by saying the words. So poems make you imagine a lot of little pictures, one after another.

Poems are written in verses. When you are writing a story, you write in sentences. But verses are in short lines. These short lines help you to get the rhythm.

Poems are like songs and music with pictures in your mind. Read this poem. See if you can hear the rhythm and see the pictures in your mind.

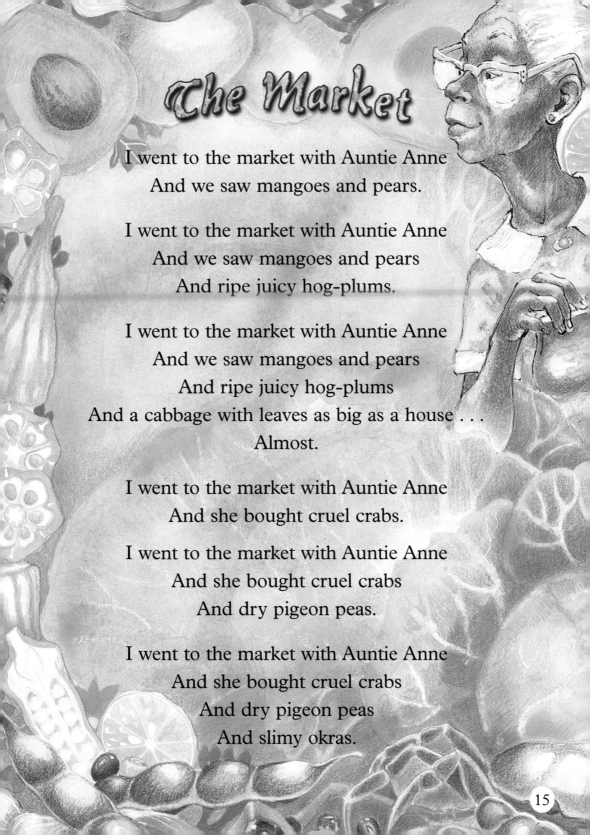

The Market

I went to the market with Auntie Anne
And we saw mangoes and pears.

I went to the market with Auntie Anne
And we saw mangoes and pears
And ripe juicy hog-plums.

I went to the market with Auntie Anne
And we saw mangoes and pears
And ripe juicy hog-plums
And a cabbage with leaves as big as a house . . .
Almost.

I went to the market with Auntie Anne
And she bought cruel crabs.

I went to the market with Auntie Anne
And she bought cruel crabs
And dry pigeon peas.

I went to the market with Auntie Anne
And she bought cruel crabs
And dry pigeon peas
And slimy okras.

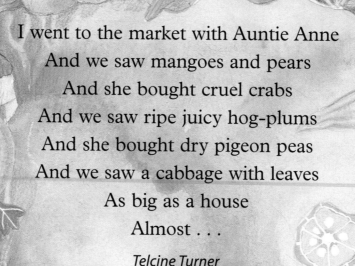

I went to the market with Auntie Anne
And we saw mangoes and pears
And she bought cruel crabs
And we saw ripe juicy hog-plums
And she bought dry pigeon peas
And we saw a cabbage with leaves
As big as a house
Almost . . .

Telcine Turner

ACTIVITIES

Language Skills

1 Read the poem and find the words that are repeated in the verses.

2 Pick out the words that come close together which start with the same letters or sounds.

3 Talk about the pictures that you imagined when you read this poem. What words made you see these pictures?

4 What did you imagine when you read about the cabbage? What word made you know that the cabbage wasn't as big as you thought?

Creativity

5 Draw a funny picture of the cabbage or the crabs.

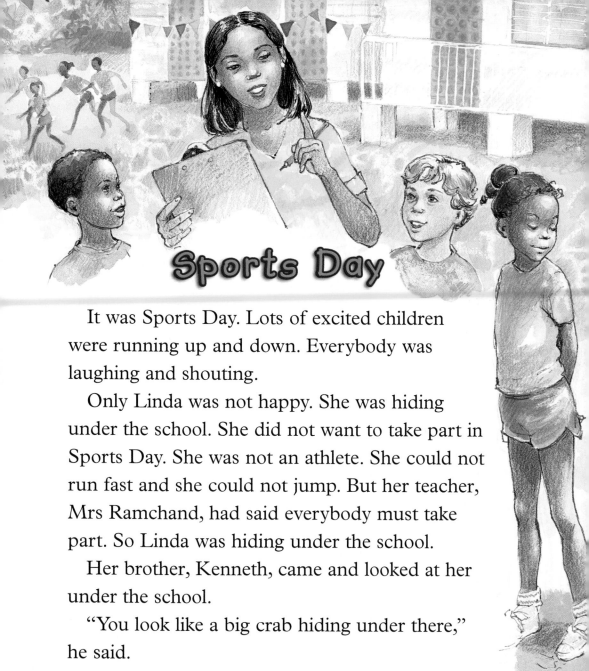

Sports Day

It was Sports Day. Lots of excited children were running up and down. Everybody was laughing and shouting.

Only Linda was not happy. She was hiding under the school. She did not want to take part in Sports Day. She was not an athlete. She could not run fast and she could not jump. But her teacher, Mrs Ramchand, had said everybody must take part. So Linda was hiding under the school.

Her brother, Kenneth, came and looked at her under the school.

"You look like a big crab hiding under there," he said.

Linda quickly started to crawl away but he grabbed one of her feet. She pulled and pulled but he would not let go.

"Come on, Crab, don't crawl away," he said. "Mrs Ramchand says you are to come and help her."

"Tell her I am not coming," said Linda.

"You can't tell her that," her brother said. "You had better come before she comes for you."

Linda crawled sadly out from under the school. She walked as slowly as she could towards Mrs Ramchand. Mrs Ramchand smiled at her.

"Please come and help me judge some of these races, Linda."

Linda was happy to hear that she did not have to race. She smiled.

"Yes, Mrs Ramchand," she said.

It was great fun being a judge. From where she was sitting, she could see everything. She got very excited when children from her class were in a race. She jumped up and shouted like all the others. Sometimes she almost forgot she was a judge.

Then it was time for the market basket race. This was a race for boys and girls. Mrs Ramchand came running up to her.

"The boy from our class is not here for this race," she said. "What are we going to do?"

"Let me do it," Linda said quickly. She was very excited.

Mrs Ramchand smiled a big smile. "Good girl," she said.

Linda ran to the starting line. This race was more like a walking race. You had to pick up some fruits, one by one, and put them in a basket. Then you had to put the basket on your head and get to the finish without holding the basket.

The race started and Linda picked up the fruits as fast as she could. Then she put the basket on her head and moved off. She did not look at the others. She did not want to rock the basket on her head.

"Come on, Crab," Kenneth shouted. "Move a little faster!"

Linda moved a little faster. The basket rocked a little. One basket dropped behind her. Everybody shouted.

One basket dropped right in front of her. Everybody laughed.

Linda could see the finish coming up. She could see Mrs Ramchand laughing. Only one boy was in front of her. He was nearly running. Then suddenly his basket dropped to the ground, BUFF! Linda laughed.

As she laughed her basket started to rock. It rocked to the right and Linda turned her head to the left.

Her basket rocked to the left and Linda turned her head to the right.

"Come on, Crab," shouted Kenneth.

Rock to the right. Turn to the left.

"Come on, Linda," shouted Mrs Ramchand.

Rock to the left. Turn to the right.

BUFF! The basket dropped.

But as it dropped Linda pushed her neck right out. The basket dropped over the finish line. She was first!

Linda jumped and shouted. Mrs Ramchand came up to her laughing and clapping.

"Very good, Linda," she said. "You came first!"

"Yes. That was fun," Linda said. "I like Sports Day. I would like it even if I didn't win."

Kenneth ran up and clapped Linda on the back.

"That was great, Crab," he said, laughing. "Next year I will send you to the Crab Olympics. You will be sure to win a gold medal!"

ACTIVITIES

Comprehension

1 Why was Linda not happy at the beginning of Sports Day?

2 How did Kenneth show he was cross with Linda for not taking part in Sports Day?

3 Why did Kenneth call his sister a crab?

Literature

4 Would you like to have a brother like Kenneth? Say why.

Reading strategies

5 On what page would you find sentences that tell you:
   a) How Linda behaved when she was a judge?
   b) How Linda crawled from under the school?
   c) In which direction the basket rocked?

Comprehension and Language

6 Pretend you are Linda and your basket has fallen and you have not won. What would:
   a) Mrs Ramchand have said to you?
   b) Kenneth have said to you?
   c) You have said?

Sporting Events

In your last story Kenneth made a joke by saying
Linda could go to the Crab Olympics. Of course,
there is no Crab Olympics. But there is a sporting
event called the Olympic Games. All the countries
in the world can take part. The Olympic Games
are held every four years. Each time they are held
in a different country. The Olympic Games go on
for weeks. Athletes take part in all kinds of sports.
Athletes from the West Indies go to the Olympic
Games. Our athletes are well known. Many have
won gold medals for coming first in their events.

There are other sporting events besides the Olympic Games. People in all countries play all kinds of sports. Sometimes countries compete against each other. The different countries in the West Indies compete against each other also. But sometimes they get together to compete against other countries in the world. Cricket is one of the sports where they do this. The West Indies cricket team is well known in the world.

Athletes have to practise and do a lot of exercise. Sports are a way for us to exercise. Exercise helps to keep us healthy. So sports are fun and they keep us healthy. What sport do you like best?

ACTIVITIES

Comprehension

1 What are the Olympic Games?
2 How often are they held?
3 What is a game in which the West Indies competes with other countries?
4 Give two reasons why sports are good for us.

Study Skills

5 Find out the name of one sport in which the countries of the West Indies compete against each other.
6 Do a class project to collect pictures of West Indian sports figures. Decide how you are going to display them and label them.

Why the Rain Bird Calls the Rain

Long ago after the Great Father had created the birds and given them their beautiful colours he sent them a message. He needed all the birds to come to him because he had a job for them. Most of the birds flew to him eagerly, happy to help.

"What can we do for you, Great Father?" they sang.

"Is it something even I can help you with?" asked the little Peewee.

"Oh yes!" said the Great Father. "It is something even the little hummingbird can help me with."

"Oh I do wish I were a bird, so that I could help the Great Father," croaked the little frog. "Don't worry, one day you will," smiled the Great Father.

The Great Father looked and saw that all his birds had come except the Cuckoo. He waited for a while and then he saw the Lizard Cuckoo and the Chestnut Bellied Cuckoo slowly approaching. They had come last because they were lazy and did not wish to do any work.

The Great Father knew this but he said nothing. He just waited until they were gathered with the others. Then he explained what he wanted the birds to do.

"The waters that fall when I send the rains do not know where to go. Because of this they cause great destruction. Some should flow down to the sea as streams and rivers. Some should gather in hollows and form lakes and some should burrow beneath the earth so that there will be water for the roots of the trees when there is no rain. I need you birds to show the waters how to flow properly."

"Oh we will be so happy to do this," chorused the birds. All, that is, except the Cuckoos.

"Why can't the waters learn to make their own way?" they demanded. "It is easy enough. No one showed us how to fly or search for food."

"No one tells you how to raise your own children either," the Great Father reminded the lazy Cuckoos.

"Look, let whoever needs water help the rainwater to find its way," they said.

The other birds stood in wonder. How could the Cuckoos speak to the Great Father like that? Surely they would be punished. They whispered to each other.

The Great Father turned to the other birds. "You can all go. Show my water how to reach where it needs to be. If you don't show it how to take its time it will wash away the land and drown the plants and animals. All will know how you helped me. After the rains fall, I will take the bowl that held the paints I used to colour you and hang it in the sky."

The birds hurried off. They flew in different directions, fluttering this way and that through the land. They showed the waters how to gurgle between the walls of gashes in the earth, creating rivers. They showed the waters how to skip over rocks and jump over steep cliffs, creating great thundering waterfalls. The little Toddy showed the water how to burrow beneath the earth and hide in caves till it was needed. Other birds showed the water where the hollows were so that it could gather there and form lakes.

After the other birds had gone, the Great Father turned to the lazy Cuckoos. "You have to be punished," he said. "You need to learn not to be so selfish and lazy. So from now on you will not be allowed to drink water from rivers or lakes. When you are thirsty you must find rainwater that has

gathered in hollow rocks or trees. The Cuckoos were not worried and flew off.

But, in the dry months, when the earth is parched and dusty and the sun colours the grasses brown, the Cuckoos know what it means to be thirsty. As the hollows that held pools of water dry up they beg the Great Father to send rain. All over the land you can hear their hoarse prayers. That is why our cuckoos are known as rain birds, because the ever-forgiving Great Father always hears their prayers and sends the rains.

By Jean Forbes

ACTIVITIES

Comprehension
1 Tell what happened in this story.

Language Skills
2 The Great Father says, "The waters that fall when I send the rains do not know where to go. Because of this they cause great **destruction**."
   a) Write in your own words what you think the word in **bold** means.
   b) Now look up the meaning of the word in the dictionary. Was your meaning correct?
3 Look at the birds that come into your school yard or at your home. Write about one. What does it look like? What is it doing?

Rain

The rain is raining all around,
It falls on field and tree,
It rains on umbrellas here,
And on the ships at sea.

Robert Louis Stevenson

everybody he knew that he was going to be
a mechanic some day.

Suddenly he stopped. He looked at the wheels of
the bus. He stared at them. One of the wheels
looked different from the others. It looked as if
something was wrong with it. But before he could
think, or say, or do anything, Miss Jones, their
teacher, called him.

"Come on, Jerry!" she shouted. "Time to go."

Jerry jumped into the bus and sat next to Roy in the back. Everybody was having a good time. But Jerry could not stop thinking about the wheel. He was sure that something was wrong with it.

Roy looked at Jerry. "What's wrong with you?" asked Roy. "Are you feeling sick? You look terrible."

"No," replied Jerry, "but something is wrong with one of the wheels."

"What are you talking about?" said Roy. "Mr Henry is a good driver. He would know if there was something wrong with one of the wheels."

All their other friends at the back wanted to know what was wrong. So Jerry told them about the wheel. He told them that he was going to ask Mr Henry to stop the bus.

"What!" said Karla. "You are only a little boy. You can't tell Mr Henry, the driver, to stop the bus. Everybody will laugh at you."

Then Patsy said, "You are not a mechanic yet, you know. If you stop this bus perhaps Miss Jones will get angry. Then she will take us back home. You'll spoil the picnic."

Jerry thought about what his friends had said. He did not want to get into trouble. He did not want everybody to laugh at him. And he did not want to spoil the picnic.

Perhaps his friends were right. He was just a little boy. If something was wrong, Miss Jones and Mr Henry would know. But then he thought about it again. Suppose he was right! He had to do something. Jerry jumped up to go to the front of the bus. His friends grabbed him, shouting, "Stop, Jerry! Don't spoil the picnic!"

With all the shouting and jumping up and down, and the pushing and pulling, Mr Henry had to stop the bus.

"What is this?" said Miss Jones. "Are you children mad?" Then she saw Jerry's face. "Are you feeling sick, Jerry?" she asked.

"No, Miss," said Jerry. "I just wanted to tell Mr Henry to stop the bus. There is something wrong with one of the wheels."

"Something wrong?" said Miss Jones. "You are just a little boy. What do you know about wheels?"

"Something wrong," said the children in the bus. Some of them started to laugh. But Miss Jones did not laugh. She stared at Jerry. She was very angry.

But when Miss Jones looked at Jerry's face she could see that he was not playing a trick. "What do you think, Mr Henry?" she said. "Could anything be wrong with one of the wheels?"

"Of course not," said Mr Henry, "but I'll have a look and then we'll all feel better."

Mr Henry walked around the bus. The children watched him as he went from wheel to wheel. Suddenly he gave a shout. Everybody jumped out of the bus to see what was wrong.

"Jerry is right," said Mr Henry. "Something is wrong with this wheel. It does not fit properly. It looks as if one of the mechanics put the wrong nuts on it. The wheel would have come off. So it's the right wheel but the wrong nuts. That mechanic did not do his work properly. It's a good thing that Jerry noticed the wheel."

"What do we do now, Mr Henry?" said Miss Jones.

"You can still go on the picnic," he replied. "I'll call for another bus. And this time Jerry and I will look at all the wheels before we start. He is going to be a good mechanic some day," said Mr Henry with a smile.

ACTIVITIES

Comprehension

1 How did the children show they were excited?

2 Why did Jerry not get in the bus right away?

3 Why did the children ask Jerry not to tell the grown-ups about the wheel?

4 a) How do you think Jerry felt after Mr Henry spotted the faulty wheel?
   b) Why do you think he felt like that?

5 a) What would you have done if you were Jerry?
   b) Why would you have done that?

6 What might have happened if Jerry had not seen the wheel?

Language

7 Read the first paragraph of the story again. List words of 2 syllables, e.g. pic nic . If there are any words of more than 2 syllables, write them down too.

There are many different ways of sending a
message. One way of sending a message is to write
a note. Another way is to use the telephone. But if
you want to keep your message a secret from other
people, you can use a code. A code is a special way
of sending a message.

The Morse Code

People all over the world know the Morse Code.
It was made up by a man named Samuel Morse. In
the Morse Code, dots and dashes stand for
different letters of the alphabet.

A ∘ —	H ∘ ∘ ∘ ∘	O — — —	V ∘ ∘ ∘ —
B — ∘ ∘ ∘	I ∘ ∘	P ∘ — — ∘	W ∘ — —
C — ∘ — ∘	J ∘ — — —	Q — — ∘ —	X — ∘ ∘ —
D — ∘ ∘	K — ∘ —	R ∘ — ∘	Y — ∘ — —
E ∘	L ∘ — ∘ ∘	S ∘ ∘ ∘	Z — — ∘ ∘
F ∘ ∘ — ∘	M — —	T —	? ∘ ∘ — — ∘ ∘
G — — ∘	N — ∘	U ∘ ∘ —	full stop ∘ — ∘ — ∘ —

You can make the dots and dashes in many different ways. You can make them with sounds or lights. This is why Morse is such a useful code.

Try sending a message yourself. Tap your foot on the floor. This is a dot. Scrape your foot along the floor. This is a dash. Now, using taps and scrapes (dots and dashes), signal your name.

There are some signals in Morse Code that are very well known. The letters S.O.S. are a special signal for help all over the world. The S.O.S. signal is made by three short dots, then three long dashes, then three short dots again: • • • ▬ ▬ ▬ • • •

Use taps and scrapes to signal an S.O.S. message.

ACTIVITIES

Comprehension

1 What is a code?

2 What do you think are some of the reasons why people use codes?

Language

3 **Remember**, after a short vowel, double the consonant before adding **ing**, e.g. plan + [n] + **ing** = **planning**
Add 'ing' to each of the words below:

| plan | bet | dig | shop | run | begin |

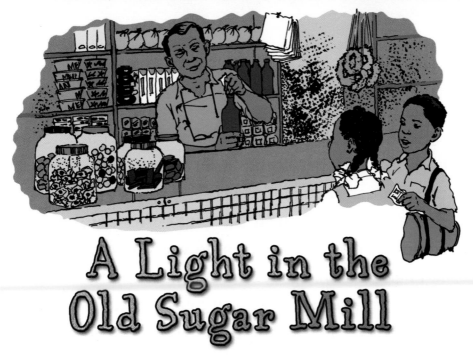

A Light in the Old Sugar Mill

Part I

Sarah and Peter were going home from school. They stopped at Mr Chin's shop to buy some matches and some kerosene for their mother. Mr Chin put the oil in a bottle. Then he put a thick bit of paper into the mouth of the bottle to make a stopper. Peter pushed the bottle into his school bag and the children walked quickly down the road as they wanted to get home before dark. They had not gone far, when they heard a sound. The children stopped to listen. They heard the sound again.

"Maa, maa."

"It's a little goat," said Peter.

"It sounds as if it is in trouble," said Sarah. "Let us look for it."

So the children left the road and went into the bush to see if they could find the little goat. But even though they looked everywhere they could not find it. They could hear the goat's cries but they could not tell where the sound was coming from.

Then suddenly they saw the walls of an old sugar mill. They had not noticed it before because it was almost hidden by thick bushes and trees. Some of the trees hung over the walls.

The children ran towards the building. They thought that the goat must be hidden somewhere in the bushes growing around it.

But even though they looked everywhere they still could not find the little goat.

Then the goat cried again, "Maa, maa."

"It's inside the building," said Peter.

"But how did it get inside?" asked Sarah.

They walked around the building, and at last they noticed that the wall was broken in one place where the old door used to be. Although there were stones blocking this opening now, there was a space there where the stones had broken away. The children climbed up on some stones which were against the wall and looked through the opening.

There were bushes and trees growing inside the building also. The trees on the outside which hung over the walls made it seem dark at first. But soon they saw a little brown goat, on the ground. It looked back at them with big sad eyes and cried, "Maa, maa."

"It must have climbed through this space," said Sarah. "But one of its legs seems to be broken. That's why it could not climb out again."

Quickly Sarah and Peter climbed through the
opening in the wall and jumped down.

"I'll climb up again," said Peter. "Then you can
give me the goat. After it is safe on the ground
outside, I will help you up."

Peter was about to climb back through the
opening, when suddenly the stones began to move.

"Look out, Peter!" shouted Sarah. "Jump!"

Just in time, Peter jumped back from the wall.

One by one, stones from around the opening

fell to the ground. Then more stones fell. Some fell
to the ground at the children's feet. But others fell
into the space in the wall.

The space they had climbed through was no
longer there. There was now just a very small
opening, not big enough for a child or a goat to
climb through. They looked around the building.
There were no other openings in the walls. Just like
the goat, they were trapped in the old mill.

Part II

"We will have to call for help," said Peter. "Somebody must hear us. After all, we heard the goat."

So they called out. They called one at a time. Then both children shouted for help. Again and again they shouted. But no one seemed to hear them, and it was getting dark.

"If we had a light," said Peter, "we could signal a message for help through the hole in the wall. Remember we learned about the Morse Code. Even though people are too far away to hear us, they could still see the light flashing."

"But we do have a light," replied Sarah. "We have the bottle with the kerosene oil and we have matches. We can make a bottle torch."

Peter got the bottle and turned it over so that the kerosene oil ran on to the thick stopper. Then he used the matches to light the stopper.

He flashed the bottle torch quickly from side to side against the hole to give three short flashes of light through the hole. Then he moved it slowly from side to side against the hole to give three longer flashes of light. Then he moved it quickly again.

"That is the code for help," said Peter.

"I hope other people know that," said Sarah.

Sarah watched as Peter flashed the bottle torch again and again; three times quickly, three times slowly, and three times quickly.

Then, just when they were almost about to give up hope, they heard a sound. It was the sound of people calling out.

"We are trapped inside the old sugar mill," the children shouted.

The people called back to the children. Soon they could hear the people just outside the walls.

Then they saw a light up in a tree. A man was climbing in one of the trees which hung over the walls.

"Tie this around you," he shouted, as he threw one end of a rope down to them.

Peter tied the rope around Sarah, and the man pulled her slowly up into the tree. Next, Peter tied the rope around the goat, and the man pulled up the little goat who cried, "Maa, maa." Then it was Peter's turn. At last they were all safe.

Peter's friend, Trevor, was with the men.

"It's a lucky thing we learned that code in school," he said. "I saw the light flashing and knew what it was."

"It's a good code to know. Don't you think so, little goat?" said Sarah.

ACTIVITIES

Comprehension

1 The children were lucky that they had certain things with them which they could use to call for help. What were these things?

Language

2 **Remember**, when you are changing a verb to the past tense, after a short vowel, double the consonant, e.g. tap + $\boxed{p}$ + ed = **tapped**.
Add 'ed' or 'd' to each of the words below.

stop....   hop....   pat....
rob....   stir....   occur....
shape....   hope....   rope....

Creativity

3 a) Draw a picture to show one part of the story that you liked.
  b) Choose sentences from the story that will describe your picture. Write the sentences below your picture.

What is a Robot?

A robot is a machine that can work by itself. It can do many of the things that people do. Most robots work in factories. Many motor car factories use robots to help make motor cars. They can do some kinds of work better than people, because they are strong and quick. They can work all day and not get tired.

Some robots are made with hands and fingers to do things like people. Some people say that one of these days robots will be able to do all the work that people do. Then people will not have to work so hard.

But children will still have to go to school. Robots will not be able to learn for us.

ACTIVITIES

Comprehension

1 Why can robots do some work better than people?

2 Why do you think robots will not be able to learn for us?

Spelling

3 How many words can you make from the word 'robot'? 'Boot' is one. See if you can find five others.

The Birthday Robot

Ravi got a robot for his birthday. His uncle in Canada sent it for him. At first he did not know what it was. Then his father told him it was a toy robot. He said a real robot was a machine that could do a lot of things by itself.

Ravi's robot was a funny looking thing. It looked something like a man but the head was like a box. It did not have any nose or mouth. The eyes were big and round. It had two things sticking out of the top of its head. It had arms and hands but it had only two fingers. They were not really like fingers. They looked more like claws. It did not have feet. It had two wheels where the feet should be.

Ravi pushed a button at the back of the robot. Right away they heard noises inside it: click – click – click! click – click – click! Red and green lights started to flash inside the eyes. The hands started to move up and down. Then the wheels started to turn and the robot moved forward.

Ravi laughed.

"Let us see what it will do now," said his father.

The robot moved clicking along. Its eyes were flashing. Then after it had gone a little way it stopped. The hands went down and the claws opened. A piece of paper was right in front of the robot. The claws grabbed the paper. Then the robot turned around and rolled and clicked right back to where it had started.

The claws opened and it dropped the piece of paper. The clicking stopped and the lights went off. Ravi laughed and clapped.

"What a great little robot!" he said.

Ravi was most excited about his robot. He had it rolling and clicking and grabbing things all morning. He could tell just how far it would go before the claws opened and it grabbed something. It was great fun.

Then he started to get into trouble with it. First he put it on the table where he tried to make it lift a cup and the robot dropped it. Luckily it did not break.

"If it wasn't your birthday you would find out something," his father said. Ravi laughed but he did not let his father see him laughing.

After lunch his mother was tired. She went to rest for a while on the bed. Ravi put the robot near her head. The robot rolled forward and grabbed her hair in its claws. His mother screamed and sent the robot flying off the bed. Luckily it did not break.

"If it wasn't your birthday you would find out something," his mother said. Ravi laughed but he did not let his mother see him laughing.

He went outside. His sister was sitting on the step. She was going to eat a banana. Ravi asked her for a piece.

"No," she said. "You just ate one." Just then her mother called her.

"If you touch that banana I will tell on you," Ravi's sister said to him. She left the banana on the step and went inside. Ravi pressed the button on the robot. Click – click – click . . . The robot rolled forward and picked up the banana. Then it came back and dropped the banana on a piece of paper Ravi put on the ground. His sister came back just as Ravi was running away.

"Ravi," she screamed. "Where is my banana? I am going to tell on you!"

"But I didn't touch it," Ravi said. "The robot touched it!" He laughed and pushed the banana into his mouth.

It was the best birthday he had ever had. That night he slept with the robot beside his head. As he slept he dreamed. In his dream, the robot was a giant. The click – click – click was as loud as a jet plane. The flashing lights were as bright as the sun. The claws were giant claws.

The robot was running after Ravi with its claws going up and down. Ravi was trying to run but he could not move. And he was turning into a banana.

Click – click – click . . . click – click – click . . . The robot's giant claw grabbed him by his hair. Ravi, the banana, screamed.

"Help!"

As he screamed he woke up. His mother woke up and came running into the room.

"What is it? What is it?" she said.

Ravi looked down at his robot. It looked so little beside his bed.

"It was the robot," he said. "It was running after me!" His mother laughed.

"I am not surprised," she said. "Don't make so much trouble with it tomorrow!"

Ravi smiled. "All right," he said. He turned over and went back to his dreams.

ACTIVITIES

Comprehension

1 What trouble did Ravi cause with his robot?

2 How did his dream fit in with the day he had spent?

3 Why was Ravi frightened by his dream?

4 What made Ravi feel better after he awoke from his dream?

5 How do you know he felt better?

Language

6 **Remember**, when 'all' is joined to a word or syllable, it drops an 'l', e.g. al 𝕝 + so = **also**. When 'full' is added to a word, it too drops an 'l'.

Add **'all'** in front of each of these words:

so	ways	most	ready	together

Add **'full'** after each of these words:

hope	shame	joy	dread	help

59

Shoes have Tongues

Shoes have tongues
But cannot talk
Tables have legs
But cannot walk.

Needles have eyes
But cannot see,
Chairs have arms
But they can't hug me!

ACTIVITIES

Comprehension and Language
What am I?

I have four legs.	I am an animal.
I can't run.	I am a pet.
You can sleep in me.	I can climb trees.
I am a	I am a ....

Make up two riddles of your own.

The People I Know Collect Funny Things

The people I know
Collect funny things
Like ships and shoes and bits of string.

Mum collects furry, fringed mats
In different shapes and colours.
Gran collects weird, wild hats
With feathers and faded flowers.
Dad collects screws and nails and keys for locks
From the house where we lived before.
Gran'pa collects purple plastic pails for rocks
He finds along the sea shore.

Who collects funny things
Like ships and shoes and bits of string?
Nobody I know.

Collecting Stamps

Lots of people used to collect stamps. Today many people write to each other by email but before we had email people usually had to post letters. Imagine all the people in the world posting letters! Stamps have all kinds of pictures from the different countries on them. No wonder people liked collecting stamps.

The countries in the West Indies have a lot of interesting stamps. There are stamps showing athletes, plants, animals and places in the different countries. There are stamps with pictures of people who did important things. Do you know anybody who still collects stamps?

ACTIVITIES

Language Skills

1 Find all the words from the poem that made you imagine pictures. Write them in your journal or portfolio. Draw pictures of some of them.

Study Skills

2 Do a class project: Try to find stamps from your own country and from the rest of the West Indies. Put them into groups by countries. Then put them into groups by the picture that is on them, such as animals, plants, interesting people and places.

Stamp Hunting

The children looked at their grandfather with long faces. There were Peter, and Marlon, and Jennifer and Betty. And then there was little Debbie. The rain was pouring down outside.

"We can't go to dancing," said Jennifer and Betty.

"We can't play cricket," said Peter and Marlon.

Debbie said nothing. The others usually said she was too little. So they would not take her with them or let her play their games.

"The rains have started," said their grandfather. "So you might as well find something to do in the house. There are other things besides dancing and cricket. What about stamp hunting?"

"You mean stamp collecting," said the girls. "That's no fun!"

"Stamp collecting," said the boys. "That's boring!"

"No!" said their grandfather. "Not stamp collecting. We are going to start with stamp hunting. You have relatives in many different countries. There must be lots of old letters from them around. See how many different stamps you can find. This is an old house so you will have to hunt for them. I will give two prizes." He went on, "One will be for the oldest and one for the most interesting stamp. Now, get set, go! On with the stamp hunt!"

Off went the four older children with screams and shouts. They looked on top of Grandfather's desk. They opened the desk drawers. They looked in Grandmother's workbasket. They looked in the drawers in all the rooms in the house. They hunted through boxes under the beds.

Debbie ran behind them. But they found all the old letters first. After a time the four older children had a good collection of stamps. Little Debbie had only one.

The other children showed Grandfather their collection. They had stamps from most of the islands. There were stamps with birds from Barbados, stamps with athletes from Jamaica, and stamps with flowers from Trinidad and Tobago. There were even stamps with fish from the Cayman Islands. And they had stamps from Guyana, and the United States and Canada.

"They are very pretty," said Grandfather. "It will be hard to decide which is the most interesting. But they are not very old. You know one of the most valuable stamps in the world comes from Guyana. You may not find anything so old, or so valuable. But look again."

Debbie's stamp was from Jamaica. It was a pretty red and orange stamp of an Arawak Indian. But she had found it on the table in Grandmother's room. So she knew it was not old.

The other children decided to look in the room at the back of the house. It had lots of old things so it must have lots of old stamps. Debbie wanted to go too but the others laughed at her.

"It's dark in there," said Betty and Jennifer. "You'll be frightened."

"There are rats in there to bite you," said Peter.

"And spiders to crawl on you," said Marlon.

Debbie did not like rats or spiders. So she decided to go and look at the cars driving through the rain.

65

But she was too little to see out of the window. So she climbed up on the table under the window. The table was next to the old bookcase.

The table swayed. It touched the bookcase. The bookcase swayed. The books on top of the bookcase moved. Debbie was frightened. She hoped the bookcase would not fall over. She started to climb down.

Her feet were almost on the ground when the table touched the bookcase again. The bookcase swayed. The books on top fell to the ground. Bang! Bang! Debbie hoped that nobody had heard. Quickly she started to pick up the books.

Suddenly an old letter fell out of one of the books. There was a stamp on it that looked like the one she had found. Then as she looked at it again she saw that it was a little different. Debbie was excited. She ran to Grandfather shouting, "Look what I have found!"

Everybody came to see what Debbie had found. She held up her two stamps.

"What! You have only two stamps," laughed the girls.

"And they are the same," said the boys.

"No, they are not!" shouted Debbie.

"Debbie is right," said Grandfather. "They look the same but one is very old. It is from the time when I was a boy. The other is new. It has been printed again. And it has the new cost of the stamp printed in black over the old cost. This is most interesting. Debbie has found the oldest stamp and also the most interesting stamp. She gets both prizes."

"How did you ever find those stamps?" asked the other children.

"Oh, it was nothing," said Debbie. "I just knew where to look."

This is a true story.

ACTIVITIES

Comprehension

1 Debbie said she just knew where to look for the stamps she found.
   a) Did she really know?
   b How did she find the stamps?
   c) Why did she say she knew where to look?

Study Skills

2 List all the different countries where you have family or friends. If you have an atlas, find the countries in your atlas.

Some Interesting Animals

Most of the islands of the Caribbean do not have wild animals. The most dangerous animals are found in countries where there are large forests. Guyana has large forests and so many interesting wild animals are found there.

Have you ever heard of a bushmaster or an anaconda? The bushmaster and anaconda are snakes. Many snakes in the countries where we live are not dangerous. But the bushmaster and the anaconda are both dangerous snakes.

The bushmaster is a poisonous snake and its victims die very quickly. It can be as long as five metres. Bushmasters usually travel in twos. People say that if a man kills one of these snakes, the other snake will go after him.

The anaconda can be as long as nine metres. It is not poisonous but it is very strong. This snake wraps itself around its victim to crush and kill it. Then it swallows its victim.

The biggest bushmasters and anacondas live in the forests of Guyana. But there are also smaller ones living in Trinidad.

Have you ever seen an iguana? An iguana is a lizard. There are many different kinds of lizard in the Caribbean. Most of them are very small, but the iguana is a very big lizard. It can be as long as two metres. It has spines along its back and a big strong tail. The spines make it look fierce, but it is not dangerous. The iguana can climb trees but it can also travel along the ground. It can also swim if it has to. There used to be many iguanas in places like Jamaica and the Cayman Islands. But now most of them are in Trinidad where there are still many forests.

The jaguar is a fierce animal which you can see in the forests of Guyana. It belongs to the cat family but it is very large. It looks more like a tiger than like the cats we know. The jaguar climbs trees but it also travels along the ground in the forest. It can also swim. Many animals in the forests are frightened of the jaguar because it is so fierce and strong. It usually jumps at its victim from a tree.

The ant eater is a very interesting animal. It has a big bushy tail. It uses its bushy tail to protect itself from the heat of the sun as well as from the rain. The ant eater has long jaws and a long sticky tongue. Its jaws are about sixty centimetres long. At the end of its jaws it has a little mouth. The ant eater has sharp claws. It uses its sharp claws to dig into ant hills. Then it uses its long sticky tongue to pick up the ants.

The ant eater can be as long as two metres but it does not usually trouble other animals. But if an animal troubles it, the ant eater can protect itself with its sharp claws. You find them in the forests of Guyana. The ant eater is one of the few animals that can kill a jaguar if it has to.

ACTIVITIES

Study Skills

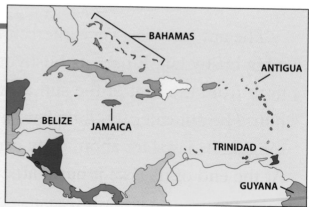

1 Get a piece of
   very thin paper
   and a pencil.
   Put the paper
   over the map.
   See how the
   map shows through the paper. Now draw round the map
   outline so that you have a copy of the map on your paper.

   Copy the names of the countries onto your map. Is your
   country named? If not, see if you can find it and name it.
   You read the names of three of the countries on pages
   68–71. Which were they? Draw a line under the three
   names on your map.

Language and Study Skills

2 Make a chart and list all the animals you read about in
   the story. Say where they live.

Animals	Where they live
Bushmaster	Guyana, Trinidad

Comprehension

3 Write down one fact about each animal that you found
   interesting in the story.

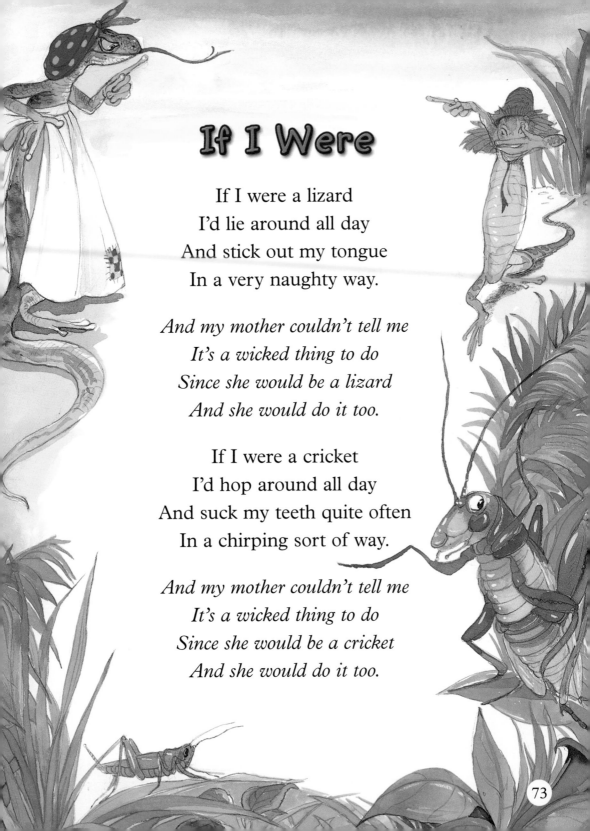

If I Were

If I were a lizard
I'd lie around all day
And stick out my tongue
In a very naughty way.

And my mother couldn't tell me
It's a wicked thing to do
Since she would be a lizard
And she would do it too.

If I were a cricket
I'd hop around all day
And suck my teeth quite often
In a chirping sort of way.

And my mother couldn't tell me
It's a wicked thing to do
Since she would be a cricket
And she would do it too.

If I were a rat bat
Then I would sleep all day
And stay awake the livelong night
In a most upsetting way.

And my mother couldn't tell me
It's a wicked thing to do
Since she would be a rat bat
And she would do it too.

If I were an earthworm
I'd play in dirt all day
And drag my feet behind me
In a lazy sort of way.

And my mother couldn't tell me
It's a wicked thing to do
Since she would be an earthworm
And she would do it too.

Pamela Mordecai

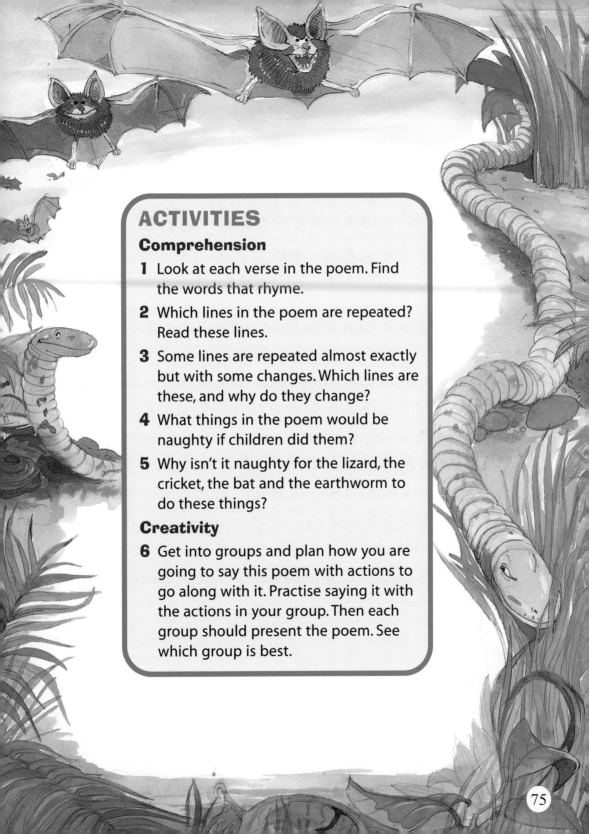

ACTIVITIES

Comprehension

1 Look at each verse in the poem. Find the words that rhyme.

2 Which lines in the poem are repeated? Read these lines.

3 Some lines are repeated almost exactly but with some changes. Which lines are these, and why do they change?

4 What things in the poem would be naughty if children did them?

5 Why isn't it naughty for the lizard, the cricket, the bat and the earthworm to do these things?

Creativity

6 Get into groups and plan how you are going to say this poem with actions to go along with it. Practise saying it with the actions in your group. Then each group should present the poem. See which group is best.

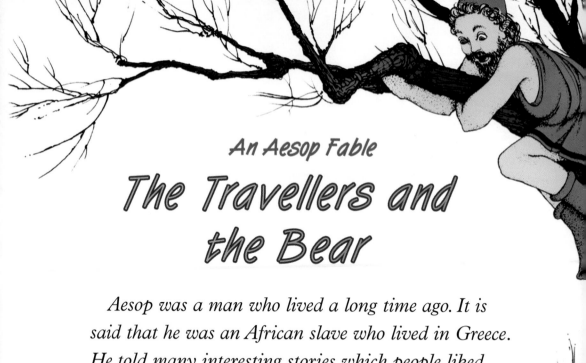

An Aesop Fable
The Travellers and the Bear

Aesop was a man who lived a long time ago. It is said that he was an African slave who lived in Greece. He told many interesting stories which people liked very much. And when he was no longer a slave he travelled to many countries where people always listened to his stories. Aesop's stories are called fables because they have a moral. Even today people tell Aesop's fables because we can learn something from the morals in them.

"The Travellers and the Bear" is one of Aesop's fables.

Once upon a time there were two friends who were travelling along a road. Suddenly they saw a bear coming towards them. They were both very frightened.

One of the travellers quickly found a tree and climbed up it to hide from the bear. He did not think of helping his friend. The other man was not able to find a tree which he could climb.

He knew that bears can be very dangerous. But he had heard that they will not trouble a dead man. So, to protect himself, he got down on the ground and pretended to be dead. He kept very still.

The bear came up to the man on the ground. It looked at him. It sniffed at his feet. It sniffed at his head. The man was very frightened but he kept very still. At last the bear walked away.

When he knew that the bear had gone, the man on the ground got up. Seeing this, the other traveller in the tree climbed down and said, "I am happy that the bear did not kill us, for a bear is usually a dangerous animal."

"Yes," said his friend. "I am happy that it did not kill me."

"But tell me," said the man who had been in the tree. "I saw the bear put its head against yours. It looked as if it was telling you something. What did it tell you?"

"This is what the bear told me," replied the other man. "It said that it is better for a man to travel alone than with a friend who is a coward. And I think that the bear is right. I will not travel with a coward." And with that he went on his way alone.

ACTIVITIES

Comprehension

1 What is a fable?
2 What is the moral of this story?
3 What facts can you find out about Aesop from the story?

Old Man Moon

The moon is very, very old
The reason why is clear
He gets a birthday once a month
Instead of once a year.

The Moonlight Monster

"What is that on the moon?" asked Donna. "It looks like the shadow of a man."

"It's a monster," said Trevor who liked to tease his little sister. "And when it is bright moonlight the monster comes down and eats up little children."

Donna's eyes were big with fright. "I don't believe you," she said with a shiver.

"Do not tease your sister, Trevor," said their mother. "You know that the shadows on the moon are the shapes of mountains and other things. But they are so far away that we cannot see them as they really are."

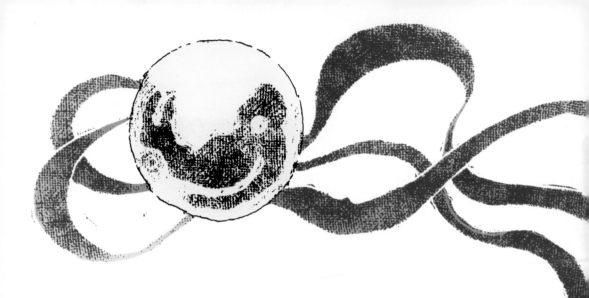

Donna looked from her mother to Trevor. She did not know which of them to believe. She knew her mother would not trick her. But the shape on the moon did not look like mountains. It looked like the shadow of a man.

As soon as their mother left the room Trevor said, "It's a monster on the moon. And on a bright moonlight night he looks out for children. If he sees any he comes down on the light and eats them."

Donna shivered again and shouted, "I don't believe you. Stop teasing me." But she was afraid.

After that Donna did not go out into the yard at night. And when she went to bed she pulled the curtains across the windows. If there was a monster on the moon she did not want him to see her.

Trevor noticed that she was afraid. So whenever their mother was not around he would tease Donna. Donna wanted to tell her mother but Trevor said, "If you tell Mummy, I will tell the moonlight monster to come down and get you. He is a friend of mine and he will do it." Donna was very unhappy.

Donna's mother did not notice what was happening. But Donna's elder sister, Beverly, knew. And she decided to do something about it.

One night Trevor was awakened by a sound. His window was open and the curtains were blowing. He could see the moon through his window but it was dark in his room.

Suddenly something came flying through the
window. Two eyes glowed in the dark. There was a
hissing sound.

Trevor sat up. He shivered. He felt as if his heart
would jump out of his mouth. The thing with the
glowing eyes went from one end of the room to the
other. It hissed and hissed. Trevor wanted to
scream, but he could not.

Then he heard a voice saying, "The moonlight
monster has come for you, Trevor. The moonlight
monster has come for you."

He could not tell where the voice came from.

Trevor knew there was no such thing as a
moonlight monster. He knew that the shadows on
the moon were the shapes of mountains.

But he did not know what was in his room. And that is why he was afraid.

Suddenly the thing with the glowing eyes jumped on his bed. He was face to face with a monster. Trevor found his voice. He screamed and screamed.

Then the thing with the glowing eyes jumped off the bed. And Trevor's mother turned on the light. Behind her was Donna. On the ground he could see their cat, who was a little wet and frightened. So that was the monster!

"What is it, Trevor?" said their mother.

"The cat woke me up," said Trevor. He felt very ashamed that he had been so afraid. "It was all over me and I didn't know what it was."

"Did you think it was the moonlight monster?" said a voice. And there was Beverly outside looking through the window.

"Of course not," said Trevor. "There is no such thing."

"Do you hear that, Donna?" said Beverly. "Trevor says there is no such thing as a moonlight monster. He has just been frightening you."

Then Beverly came inside and told their mother what had been happening. She told her how unhappy Donna had been. "I'm sorry about the cat," added Beverly as she picked it up and dried it off. "But I just had to let Trevor know what it feels like to be really afraid. So I sprinkled a little water on the cat. Then I pushed it through the window. I knew it would be frightened and that it would run around and make a noise."

"What a fright for the cat," said their mother. "But I hope Trevor has learned something from this. I'm surprised at you, Trevor!"

"Poor cat," said Donna. Then she hugged her sister.

"Thank you for helping me, Beverly," she said.

And at last Trevor could see how mean he had been to Donna. He felt very ashamed. He decided that he would have to think of a way to make it up to her.

ACTIVITIES

Comprehension

1 What do you think of the way Trevor treated Donna?

2 Say what you would have done if you were Donna.

3 How else could Beverly have helped her sister?

Study skills

4 Write the names below in alphabetical order:
Donna, Trevor, Beverly, Jerry, Sarah, Peter, Debbie, Rohan, Tiger, Indra.

Language

5 'Y' usually comes at the end of a word. When you add 'ed' or 'es' change the 'y' to 'i', e.g. bus $\boxed{y}$ + ed = **busied**.
Add **es** and **ed** to each of the words below

| carry | hurry | reply |
| study | supply | marry |

Shadow Pictures

Make some shadow pictures.

bird

Move the wings up and down.

alligator

Move the mouth up and down.

dog

Move the mouth up and down.

goat

Move the head up and down.

My Shadow

I have a little shadow that goes in and out
with me,
And what can be the use of him is more than
I can see.
He is very, very like me from the heels up to
the head;
And I see him jump before me, when I jump
into my bed.

Walter de la Mare

ACTIVITIES

Study skills

1 Find a sunny place. Put a stick in the ground. Look at the
shadow of the stick. How long is the shadow? Use your
ruler to find out how long the shadow is. Leave the
shadow an hour. How long is the shadow now? Measure
it. Leave it another hour. How long is the shadow?
Measure the shadow every hour for four hours. Write
down what you find out in a chart like this.

Time	Length of shadow
9 o'clock	
10 o'clock	

2 Now tell what you know about shadows. Did you do this
in the morning? If so, try it again in the afternoon. Did the
same thing happen?

GOING TO THE MOON

Indra and her little brother, Rohan, were sitting outside, looking at the full moon.

"The moon is pretty tonight," said Rohan. "When I get big, I am going to be a scientist and I will be the first man to go to the moon."

Indra laughed. "You can't be the first man to go, because some men have gone there already," she said. "But maybe you can be the first man from the West Indies to go to the moon."

"That would be OK," said Rohan. "When I go I will fly in a big BWIA jet. All my friends will go with me and we will have a carnival on the moon. We will dance and eat and maybe even play a Test Match against the moon-men." He was getting very excited.

Indra put back her head and laughed.

"You can't go to the moon in a plane, little brother. It is too far away for that. You have to go in a giant rocket. And as for your carnival and Test Match! I would like to see you do that on the moon!"

"Why not?" asked Rohan.

"Because the moon is not like the earth," Indra said. "The moon doesn't have any air, so people can't live there."

"But you just said some people went there already!" Rohan said.

"Yes," replied Indra, "but they had to carry air from the earth with them. And they had to wear special space-suits to protect them. The sunlight is as hot as boiling water on the moon and the darkness is colder than ice. You can't just walk around as you please!"

But Rohan was not ready to give up his moon trip yet.

"All right," he said. "But we can still have a carnival in space-suits. Nothing is wrong with that."

"Everything is wrong with it," Indra said. "People can't move about on the moon as they move about on earth. When you walk up there you are like a giant. The smallest step you take ends up like a big jump."

Rohan shook his head and yawned.

"I don't understand," he said. "Do you get bigger or something? How can you just walk like a giant?"

"It is because the moon does not have as much gravity as the earth," Indra said.

'Gravity?" said Rohan. "What is that? I don't need any gravity." He gave a big yawn.

"Of course we all

need gravity," Indra said. "If there wasn't any gravity everything would just float away into space. Gravity is a kind of power that pulls things down to the earth, and keeps them from floating away. If there wasn't any gravity, things couldn't stay in one place. The moon does not have as much gravity as the earth, so things float very easily up there. Do you understand?"

But there was no answer. Indra looked at Rohan. He was nearly asleep. Indra smiled.

"You may not need gravity, but you need your sleep, little moon-man," she said. "We can go to the moon another night."

She picked him up and carried him inside.

ACTIVITIES

Comprehension

1 What were some of Rohan's ideas about the moon that Indra had to correct?

2 a) Do you think that Indra was a good sister to Rohan?
   b) Why do you think that?

Reading strategies

3 On what page can you read about the temperature on the moon in the day and the night?

TO THE TEACHER

Word Recognition

1 Phonics – At this stage of reading ensure that each child knows the sounds represented by the digraphs: ai, ay; oa, ow, oe; oo, ew, ue; au, aw; igh, y, ie: ee, ea (e.g. p. 13, Q.3) They should have already mastered the simple vowel and consonant sounds at the earlier stages.

2 Word Building – (a) Introduce prefixes. Show children how these change the meaning of the root word. The important prefixes at this stage are: a, de, be, en, mis, in, re, un, ad, dis, pre. (b) Do the same with suffixes. Show how they change the function or tense of the root word. The important suffixes at this stage are: -ed, -er, -est, -ing, -able, -ly, -s, -ment, -y, -age, -ful (e.g. p. 51, Q.2; p. 85, Q.5). (c) Introduce words divided into syllables (e.g. p. 40, Q.7).

3 Working out meanings from context – Write sentences on the board which include a word which is not known to the children. Ask them if they can guess its meaning from the context (e.g. p. 29, Q.2). Alternatively, substitute 'nonsense words' for particular nouns or verbs, e.g. 'The **klunk's** wings beat so fast as it flew from tree to tree'. Discuss the use of a dictionary for finding meanings.

Comprehension and Literature

The questions at the end of the stories are designed to help you develop in the children different comprehension skills and the appreciation of literature. They are also designed to provide models for further questions of your own.

    (a) **Comprehension** The activities include:

        Finding the main idea and related details (e.g. p. 6, Q.2; p. 33, Q.1–4; p. 51, Q.3)

        Finding topic sentences (e.g. p. 51, Q.3)

        Organising and classifying facts (e.g. p. 78, Q.3)

        Sequencing – extract the main events or ideas from a reading passage (e.g. the water cycle sequence on pp. 31–32), present them to the children in 'mixed up' order and work out the right order in discussion.

Drawing inferences and conclusions (e.g. p. 40, Q.4, 5; p. 60;
p. 85, Q.1–3; p. 91, Q.2)
Forming judgements (e.g. p. 11, Q.1)
Predicting outcomes (e.g. p. 23, Q.6; p. 40, Q.4–6). For
some stories, break off the reading of the story at one or
two suitable points and discuss with the children what
they think might happen next (e.g. pause in the reading of
"Big for Me, Little for You", at the end of p. 11 where Tiger
has just seen all the little rabbits).
Distinguishing fact from fiction (e.g. p. 78, Q.3)
Following directions (e.g. p. 87)
(b) **Literature** The activities include:
Understanding development of plot (e.g. p. 40, Q.1–6)
Appreciating characterisation (e.g. p. 13, Q.1; p. 23, Q.4)
Inventing story and situation (e.g. p. 23, Q.6)

Language

It is important to make full use of the Reader as part of your
programme to develop the pupils' grammar, spelling and
punctuation skills and ensure their progress in all the language arts.

Understanding grammar: comparatives and superlatives (e.g. p. 13,
Q. 4); suffixes (e.g. p. 51, Q.2).
Language pattern practice – some standard English (SE) features,
e.g. present continuous tense; simple past tenses; pronouns and
various question forms, may cause problems for Creole-speaking
pupils, so use the reading material and questions to help
familiarise the children with SE conventions and reinforce
particular grammatical patterns. This need not always be a formal
exercise, for instance, the poem "The Market" on pp. 15–16 can be
played as a 'question and answer' game, with groups of children
taking it in turns to answer the questions, e.g. Question: 'I **went to**
the market with Auntie Anne and what **did we see?**' Answer: 'We
saw .....' See also p. 6, Q.3 and p. 60 – the riddles encourage
question and answer formation.
Spelling and punctuation (e.g. p. 59, Q.6; p. 85, Q.5)
Classifying (e.g. p. 33, Q.5)

Developing new vocabulary (e.g. p. 42, Q.1)
Understanding the meaning of phrases (e.g. p. 13, Q.2)
Recognising and recalling story events in sequence (e.g. p. 78, Q.3)

Using imagination in 'just suppose' situations (e.g. p. 23, Q.6).
This is also a particularly good way of familiarising the pupils with
SE conventions and practising grammatical patterns – e.g.
  (a) constructing dialogue (e.g. p. 23, Q.6)
  (b) imaginary continuation of parts of stories (e.g. p. 40, Q.6)
  (c) describing types of people, different characters, saying what
       they think the characters might do in different imaginary
       situations (e.g. p. 23, Q.6)
  (d) telling their own stories.

Study Skills
The activities include:
Recognising important details (e.g. p. 33, Q.1, 2; p. 42, Q.1, 2;
p. 52, Q.1, 2; p. 72, Q.2)
Identifying unrelated details (e.g. p. 78, Q.3)
Finding the main idea of a paragraph (e.g. p. 33, Q.3, 4; p. 52, Q.1)
Finding answers to specific questions (e.g. p. 33, Q.1, 2)
Finding information through a table of contents (see **Evaluation**)
Developing dictionary skills, e.g. alphabetical order (see p. 85, Q.4)
Following steps in sequence (e.g. p. 91, Q.1, 2)
Understanding the significance of pictorial aids (e.g. pp. 32, 86)
Reading and interpreting tables, charts, diagrams, pictures and
    maps (e.g. pp. 32, 72)
Starting to write reports on findings (e.g. p. 29, Q.1, 2)

Reading Strategies
Scanning finding a predetermined word or group of words,
    phrase, or date (e.g. p. 23, Q.5; p. 91, Q.3)
Skimming obtaining an overall impression of certain features of
    the story/text (e.g. p. 29, Q.1)

Checking written work
Help the children develop the following skills involved in checking
their written work before it is marked. They should learn to look at:

1 **Mechanics** (a) grammar; (b) spelling; (c) punctuation;
(d) capitals; (e) writing.
2 **Form** (a) Are the sentences arranged in logical order?
(b) Does each paragraph have one main idea?
3 **Meaning** (a) Is the meaning of each sentence clear? (b) Have you
used some words inaccurately?
4 **Interest** (a) Have you overused some words? (b) Have you
written sentences that are interesting to read?

Evaluation

During the year try and set work for a pupil or a group of pupils
that will assess the progress of the child in using a book. The
evaluation should cover such skills as:
1 **Using parts of a book, e.g.**
(a) On what page would you find information about Morse
Code?
(b) Where would you look to see if the book had information
about robots?
2 **Vocabulary, e.g.**
(a) What is meant by the word 'fluttering' (p. 28 line 10)?
(b) Choose the correct meaning of the word 'wonder'
(p. 27, line 21): (a) fright (b) surprise (c) worry.
3 **Comprehension**
(a) What is the main idea of paragraph 2 on p. 31?
(b) Questions to ask for specific bits of information about
characters or ideas
(c) Questions asking what may happen as a result of . . .
4 **Reading Rate**
Have the pupils note the time it takes to read a section.
Figure the reading speed in words per minute.
5 **Skimming**
2–5 questions on using skimming to find the answer for
specific questions asking for information on one page or two
pages.

Ginn & Company
Linacre House, Jordan Hill, Oxford OX2 8EJ
A part of Harcourt Education Limited

OXFORD MELBOURNE AUCKLAND
JOHANNESBURG GABORONE KUALA LUMPUR
PORTSMOUTH (NH) USA CHICAGO

First published by Heinemann Educational Publishers in 1983
This edition published 2004

ISBN 0 602 22673 2

08 07 06 05 04
10 9 8 7 6 5 4 3 2 1

British Library Cataloguing in Publication Data

A full catalogue record for this book is available from the British Library.

Design by Shireen Nathoo Design

Printed and bound in the UK by Scotprint

Visit our Caribbean Schools website at: www.caribbeanschools.co.uk